SCIENCE

THROUGH THE SEASONS

AUTUMN

GABRIELLE WOOLFITT

Wayland

Titles in the series:

Spring
Summer
Autumn
Winter

Series editor: Katie Orchard
Series designer: Pinpoint Design
Artist: Pauline Allen
Production controllers: Carol Titchener and Carol Stevens
Photo stylist: Zoë Hargreaves

First published in 1995 by Wayland (Publishers) Ltd
61 Western Road, Hove, East Sussex BN3 1JD, England

British Library Cataloguing in Publication Data
Woolfitt, Gabrielle
Autumn. – (Science Through the Seasons series)
I. Title II. Series
508

ISBN 0 7502 1460 0

Typeset in England by Dorchester Typesetting Group Ltd
Printed and bound by L.E.G.O. S.p.A., Vicenza, Italy

Cover pictures: Rosehips (left) and a red squirrel (centre).

Title page picture: A dandelion clock.

Contents

Words in **bold** are in the glossary on page 30.

What is Autumn?

During autumn, living things prepare themselves for the cold winter weather.

When it is autumn, leaves start to change colour and fall from the trees. Some plants make seeds and then die. Other plants make fruit or nuts. Birds like to eat autumn fruits and squirrels collect nuts. Some birds get ready to fly to their winter homes. Some animals prepare to **hibernate**.

◀ Bracken fern

Beech trees ▶

Red squirrel ▶

Mushrooms ▼

◀ Rosehips

In autumn, the weather changes. It gets colder and more windy. There is a lot of rain in autumn. The sun rises later and sets earlier. It remains low in the sky, even in the middle of the day. By the end of autumn, the days will be shorter and colder.

Playing among the autumn leaves that have fallen from the beech trees in this wood.

Hazel nuts ▶

Autumn Days

At the start of autumn, there is a special day called the autumn **equinox**. On this day, there are exactly twelve hours of day and twelve hours of night. The sun rises at six o'clock in the morning and sets at six o'clock at night.

During autumn, the days begin to get shorter and the nights begin to get longer. The sun stays low in the sky. The shortest day of the year is at the end of autumn. In some parts of the world, there is no daylight at all in late autumn.

(Right) Misty mornings are common in autumn.

◀ Oak

How many hours of daylight are there in autumn where you live? It can be difficult to get up in the morning if it is still dark. Sometimes you have to walk home from school in the dark. You must make sure that you wear bright clothes so that you can be seen by drivers.

Beech ▼

◄ Geese

◄ Ash

Fox ▼

If you live in Europe, the USA or Australia, your country will have four seasons, one of which is autumn. The days get shorter and colder in autumn. All the countries in the yellow parts of this globe have four seasons.

The seasons are the opposite way round in the northern and the southern **hemispheres**.
If you live in the northern hemisphere, autumn is from September to December. If you live in the southern hemisphere, autumn is from March to June.

Rosehips are a common autumn sight.
Rosehips contain seeds.

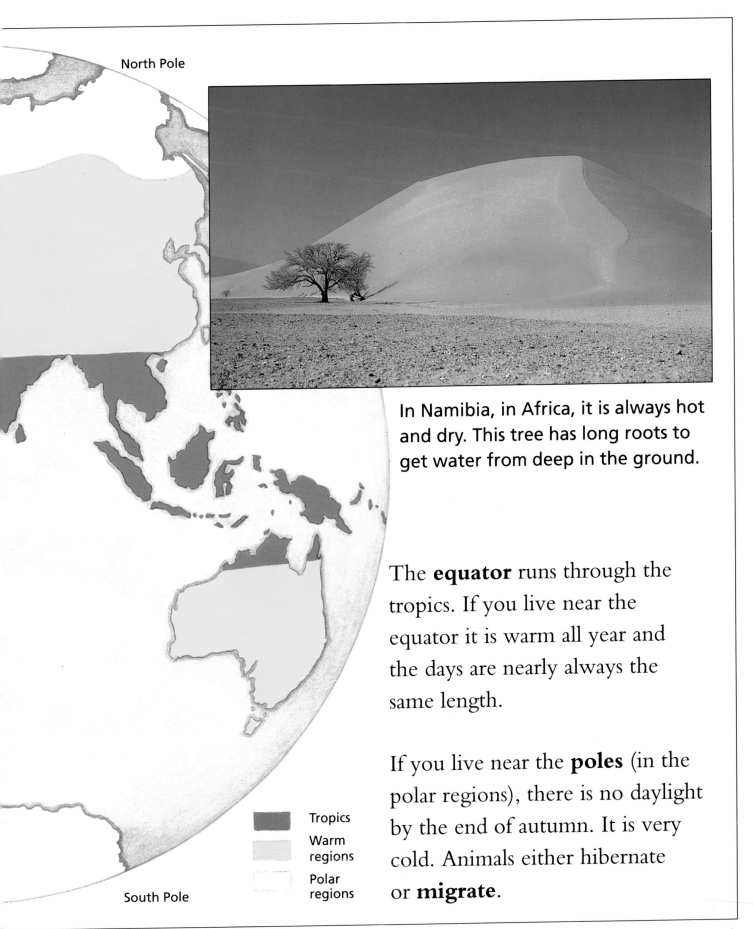

North Pole

In Namibia, in Africa, it is always hot and dry. This tree has long roots to get water from deep in the ground.

The **equator** runs through the tropics. If you live near the equator it is warm all year and the days are nearly always the same length.

If you live near the **poles** (in the polar regions), there is no daylight by the end of autumn. It is very cold. Animals either hibernate or **migrate**.

Tropics

Warm regions

Polar regions

South Pole

Autumn Weather

During the autumn months, there is usually a lot of wind and rain.

After the long, hot days of summer, the land and sea have heated up. In autumn, the heat in the land and sea rises and is lost into the air. This makes the air move about and causes storms.

A selection of autumn leaves being blown around on a windy day.

Mountain ash ▶

Wild rabbit ▶

Hazel ▶

◀ Thistle

▲ Hawthorn

◀ Silver birch

Willow ▼

▲ Maple

You can measure how windy it is using an **anemometer**. The faster it is blown around, the more windy it is. A **wind sock** can show which direction the wind is coming from. Small airports use wind socks. A **weather vane** on top of a building points in the direction the wind is going.

This is an anemometer being set up in Ellesmere, Canada.

There are two main types of trees. Trees with a round shape and flat leaves are called **deciduous** trees. **Evergreen** trees have a pointed shape and prickly leaves. This experiment shows you how different trees can cope with autumn winds.

▲ 1. Draw a pointed tree shape and a round tree shape on some cardboard. Both trees should be about 25 cm high.

YOU WILL NEED:

cardboard, a pencil or a crayon, a ruler, scissors, labels, some Plasticine, a hairdryer.

▲ 2. Cut out the trees carefully.

▲ 3. Make a mark 5 cm from the top, in the middle of each tree.

▲ 4. Stand up one tree in some Plasticine and blow the mark on the tree with air from the hairdryer.

▲ 5. Repeat with the other tree. Which shape was blown the most?

◀ 6. Make a deciduous tree without leaves by cutting out branches. Repeat the experiment and see how much it is blown now.

Without their leaves, deciduous trees are a better shape to stand up to the wind.

Autumn Rain

By the end of summer, the lack of rain has made the soil dry out. In autumn, it usually rains a lot, so the soil becomes wet again. This experiment shows you how different soils can soak up different amounts of water.

▲ 1. Put soils 1 and 2 in separate bowls. Tip each soil on to newspaper. Leave both soils in a warm, dry place for a few days.

YOU WILL NEED:

two bowls to hold soil, garden earth and potting compost (soils 1 and 2), newspaper, a large bowl, a sieve, kitchen paper.

▲ 2. Put soil 1 into a sieve lined with a piece of damp kitchen paper. Place the sieve over a bowl.

3. Pour a cup of water through soil 1. How long does the water take to go through? This tells you if water can drain quickly. See how much water comes through. ▶

▲ 4. Repeat with soil 2. Which soil can hold the most water?

Plants that need a lot of water to survive need soil that can hold water well.

Autumn Foods

Apples and blackberries are autumn fruits. Pumpkins and potatoes are autumn vegetables. These foods take several months to grow and ripen. They need lots of sunshine and water before they are ready to eat.

These apples are turning red. They will soon be ready to pick.

People collect these foods in autumn. They are stored so we can eat them in the winter when few crops grow. Potatoes should be stored in a cool, dark place. Pumpkins and apples need to be wrapped up in newspaper. Then they are put into an airy box and kept in a cool, dark shed.

Berries go mouldy once they have been picked. Berries contain Vitamin C, which helps our bodies to fight colds. To keep berries through the winter you can make jam. Can you think of other ways of **preserving** food?

Seeds, Nuts and Berries

Many plants make seeds in the autumn. Seeds grow into new plants the following year. Different plants spread their seeds in different ways.

Some seeds are light enough to be blown away by the wind. If a seed lands on soil in the autumn and survives the winter, it may grow in the spring.

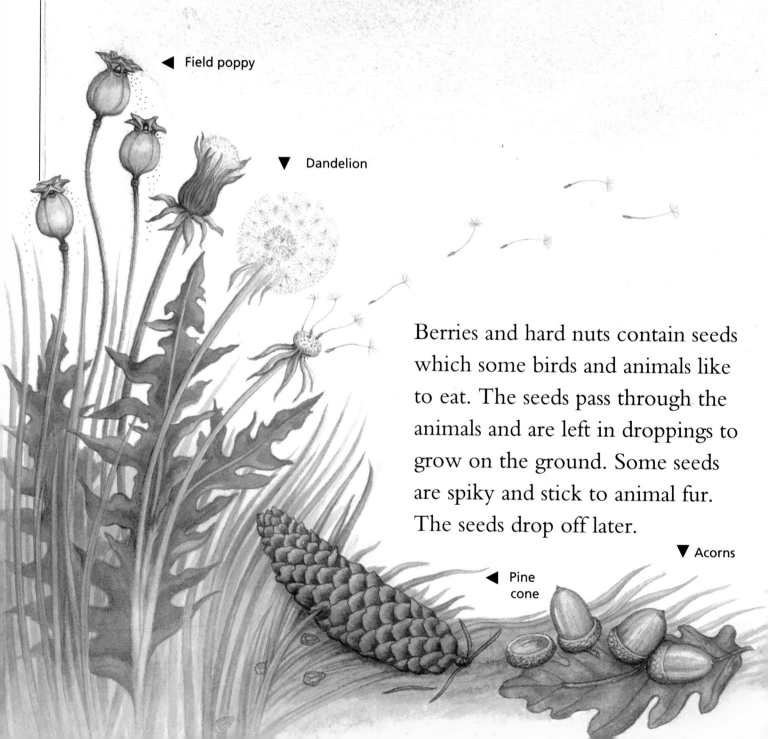

◄ Field poppy

▼ Dandelion

Berries and hard nuts contain seeds which some birds and animals like to eat. The seeds pass through the animals and are left in droppings to grow on the ground. Some seeds are spiky and stick to animal fur. The seeds drop off later.

▼ Acorns

◄ Pine cone

Maple ▲

Thrush ▶

Some nuts and seeds can float in water and may be washed on to land where they will grow.

Blackberries ▲

Rosehips ▲

(Left) This red squirrel is collecting nuts to store ready to eat in the winter. If the nuts are not eaten, they may grow where they are left.

Collecting Seeds

Autumn is a good time to find seeds. Try these experiments to see how seeds are **dispersed**.

YOU WILL NEED:
a selection of different seeds and berries, a bowl of water, a jumper, scissors, a hand-lens.

◀ 1. Hold a seed up and let it drop or blow it. Does it swirl and float around in the air?

Seeds that float or spin as they fall are dispersed by wind.

▲ 2. Put a seed on to your jumper. If it sticks, look at it with a hand-lens.

Seeds with prickles or spikes stick
to animal fur.

▲ 3. Are the seeds inside a berry?
Cut some berries in half with scissors.
Look inside for small, hard pips.

Birds eat berries. The pips are
dispersed in bird droppings.

Seeds that float can be dispersed
by water.

▲ 4. Put a seed into a bowl of water.
Does it float? Does it have a
waterproof shell?

Autumn On the Farm

Autumn on the farm is very busy. Most crops have been **harvested** at the end of summer. But there are still important jobs to do.

(Right) This tractor is ploughing the field. The birds are looking for worms and seeds in the soil that has been ploughed.

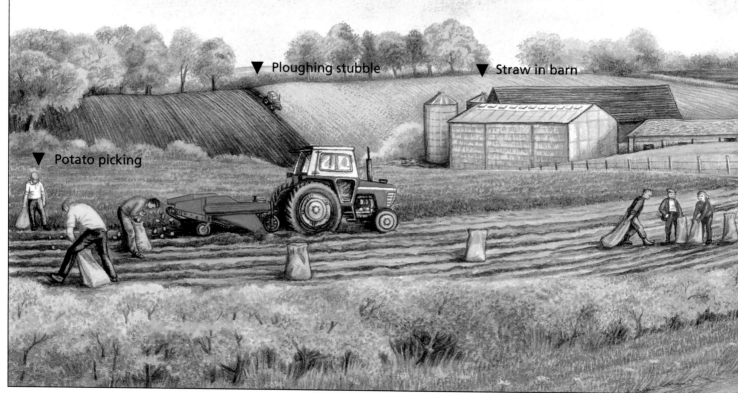

▼ Ploughing stubble

▼ Straw in barn

▼ Potato picking

The farmer ploughs the fields to chop up old plant roots. Sometimes the farmer plants quick-growing crops which are used to feed farm animals in winter. Some crops can be planted in the autumn because they can survive the cold winter. They will be ready to be harvested in spring.

Cows mostly eat grass. When it gets colder, the grass does not grow very fast. The farmer must give the cows other food to keep them fit and healthy.

In Europe, the USA and Canada, farmers fatten up turkeys in autumn. Some people eat turkeys at Christmas and Thanksgiving.

▼ Apple picking

▲ Fodder for cattle

23

Falling Leaves

In autumn, some leaves change colour, drop off the tree and rot in the ground. This experiment will help you see how leaves rot.

YOU WILL NEED:

some green leaves, paper, coloured pencils, string bags, a garden, stones.

▲ 1. Collect several types of leaves.

◀ 2. Draw the shape and colour of each type of leaf.

▲ 3. Put each leaf into a different bag. Write the name of the tree each leaf came from on light-coloured stones. Put a stone into each bag.

▲ 4. Put the bags on some earth in a garden. Put a brick or stone on top to stop the bags from blowing away.

▲ 5. After a month, check the bags. Have the leaves changed? Which leaves rotted the most? Did any not change at all? Put the bags out again and check them in another month.

Bacteria and worms in the soil help the leaves to rot. The leaves' goodness goes into the soil to be used by other plants.

Fungi

Fungi means mushrooms and toadstools. Fungi grow well in autumn. They prefer cool, damp weather. This experiment tells you more about mushrooms.

YOU WILL NEED:

five closed–cup mushrooms, coloured pencils, paper, a blunt knife, a paper bag, a plastic bag, a fridge, a chopping board, a hand lens.

NEVER TOUCH ANY FUNGI YOU FIND OUTDOORS. THEY MAY BE POISONOUS. ASK AN ADULT TO HELP YOU TO USE A KNIFE.

▲ 1. Cut one mushroom in half. Draw the outside and the inside. It might look brown under the cap.

▲ 2. Put two other mushrooms into a paper bag in a cupboard, and two into a plastic bag in a fridge.

3. After a few days take one mushroom from each bag. Cut them in halves. Notice how they have changed. Draw the inside and outside of each mushroom. ▼

▲ 4. A few days later, collect the last two mushrooms. Has the one in the fridge gone slimy? This means it has started to rot. Can you see brown **gills** on the one from the paper bag?

If you tap the dry mushroom, you might see black, powdery spores. The dry mushrooms in the paper bag will last longer than those in the plastic bag.

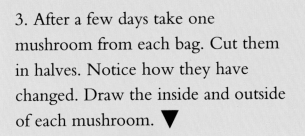

Preparing for Winter

In winter it is cold and dark. Few plants grow and animals and birds cannot find food easily. During autumn, plants and animals prepare for winter.

Swallows ▲

Deciduous trees lose their leaves in autumn so they can survive strong winds. Some plants make seeds and then die. Other plants die above the soil but keep food in roots and bulbs underground.

Some birds migrate to warmer countries. Look out for big flocks of birds preparing to fly to their winter homes.

Look closely at the fur of cats and horses. They grow a thick coat for winter. Some animals hibernate through winter. They eat as much as they can in the autumn. Some animals collect food and keep it somewhere safe to eat during the cold months ahead.

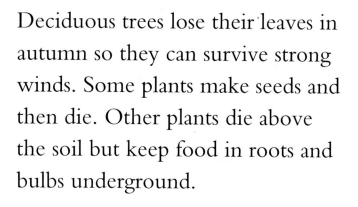

Badger ▼

▼ Dormouse   Red squirrel ▶

These red deer have grown thick winter coats to keep them warm in the snow. In the summer, their coats will look much thinner.

(Main picture) These animals are getting their winter homes ready. The badger, dormouse and hedgehog will all hibernate during winter. The squirrels and woodmouse do not hibernate, but store food to see them through the winter months. The swallows are migrating.

◀ Oak

▼ Woodmouse

▼ Hedgehog

Glossary

anemometer   An instrument that is used to measure wind. The windier it is, the more the anemometer spins round.

bacteria   Tiny plants made up of only one cell.

deciduous   Trees and bushes that lose their leaves in the winter.

dispersed   When seeds are spread so that they will grow in a new place with more room.

equator   An imaginary line around the Earth, half way between the North and South Poles.

equinox   When the day and the night are the same length. This happens twice a year.

evergreen   Plants and trees that do not lose their leaves for winter, but stay green all year.

fungi   Types of plant that are not green and grow in damp places. Mushrooms and toadstools are both fungi.

gills   Slits or flaps.

harvested   When ripe crops are gathered in.

hemispheres   The two halves of the globe. They are usually called the northern and southern hemispheres.

hibernate   To sleep for a long time during the winter.

migrate   To move to a warmer country in winter.

Poles   The place in the world that is furthest north (the North Pole), and the place that is furthest south (the South Pole).

preserving   Storing food in such a way that it does not go bad.

spores   Spores grow into new mushrooms.

weather vane   An instrument that shows wind direction.

wind sock   Shaped like a sock, this instrument points in the direction the wind is going to.

Books to Read

Autumn Weather by John Mason (Wayland, 1990)

Projects for Autumn by Joan Jones (Wayland, 1989)

Starting Ecology: Wood by Colin S. Milkins (Wayland, 1993)

Things to Make from Autumn Seeds and Leaves by Rosalie Brown
(Jade Publishers, 1989)

The World's Weather by David Flint (Wayland, 1992)

Picture Acknowledgements

Hutchison Library 5; NHPA *cover* (left),
8; Papilio 9; Scientific Photo
Library 11; Tony Stone *cover* (centre), *back cover* (bottom),
19, 22, 29; Wayland Picture Library *back cover*
(photograph by Colin S. Milkins) top left, *title
page* (photograph by Colin S. Milkins), 16; Zefa 7.

The commissioned photographs used in this book were taken
by APM Studios.

The publishers would like to thank the staff and children at
Somerhill School, Hove, Sussex, for their kind assistance.

Index